Cryptocurrency Guide For Beginners.

How To Start With Minimum Investment.

Successful Investment Strategies And How To Minimizing Your Risk. Mining, Trading, Bitcoin, Ethereum, Litecoin, ICO.

Joseph Evans

Cover image is Created by Starline - Freepik.com

FREE GIFT

I wanted to show my appreciation that you support my work so I've put together a free gift for you.

https://nb1publish.weebly.com

Just visit the link above to download it now.

Thanks!

Joseph Evans

Table of Contents

Introduction 4

History Of Cryptocurrency 8

How to Get Started 11

Advantages of Cryptocurrency 19

How to Mine Cryptocurrency 22

Things to Careful About when Mining Cryptocurrency 25

Benefits and Risks of Investing 27

Cryptocurrency Exchanges 35

List of Cryptocurrencies 44

Blockchain Technology 47

What is an ICOs and how does it work 53

Successful Investment Strategies 59

Cryptocurrency Mistakes And How To Avoid Them 65

The Future of Cryptocurrency 68

Conclusion 71

Thesaurus of Terms to Understand Cryptocurrency 72

BONUS 77

Introduction

Cryptocurrencies use cryptographic protocols, or extremely complex code systems that encrypt sensitive data transfers, to secure their units of exchange. Cryptocurrency developers build these protocols on advanced mathematics and computer engineering principles that render them virtually impossible to break, and thus to duplicate or counterfeit the protected currencies. These protocols also mask the identities of cryptocurrency users, making transactions and fund flows difficult to attribute to specific individuals or groups.

Cryptocurrencies are also marked by decentralized control. Cryptocurrencies' supply and value are controlled by the activities of their users and highly complex protocols built into their governing codes, not the conscious decisions of central banks or other regulatory authorities. In particular, the activities of miners – cryptocurrency users who leverage vast amounts of computing power to record transactions, receiving newly created cryptocurrency units and transaction fees paid by other users in return are critical to currencies' stability and smooth function.

Importantly, cryptocurrencies can be exchanged for fiat currencies in special online markets, meaning each has a variable exchange rate with major world currencies (such as the U.S. dollar, British pound, European euro, and Japanese yen). Cryptocurrency exchanges are somewhat vulnerable to hacking and represent the most common venue for digital currency theft.

Most, but not all, cryptocurrencies are characterized by finite supply. Their source codes contain instructions outlining the precise number of units that can and will ever exist. Over time, it becomes more difficult for miners to produce cryptocurrency units, until the upper limit is reached and new currency ceases to be minted altogether. Cryptocurrencies' finite supply makes them inherently deflationary, more akin to gold and other precious metals – of which there are finite supplies – than fiat currencies, which central banks can, in theory, produce unlimited supplies of.

Due to their political independence and essentially impenetrable data security, cryptocurrency users enjoy benefits not available to users of traditional fiat currencies, such as the U.S. dollar, and the financial systems, which that currencies support. For instance, whereas a government can easily freeze or even seize a bank account located in its jurisdiction, it's very difficult for it to do the same with funds held in cryptocurrency even if the holder is a citizen or legal resident.

On the other hand, cryptocurrencies come with a host of risks and drawbacks, such as illiquidity and value volatility, that don't affect many fiat currencies. Additionally, cryptocurrencies are frequently used to facilitate gray and black market transactions, so many countries view them with distrust or outright animosity. And while some proponents tout cryptocurrencies as potentially lucrative alternative investments, few (if any) serious financial professionals view them as suitable for anything other than pure speculation.

How Cryptocurrencies Work

True enough, cryptocurrency does have a long history and it has come a long way from how it started out to how it is presented and used in these modern times. But in reality, does everyone know how cryptocurrency works?

How do miners (yes, we will be explaining what miners are further on) actually make the coins and how are transactions created and verified?

To be able to have a clearer idea of how it works, it would be helpful to analyze the mechanism, which controls the databases of cryptocurrencies. Cryptocurrencies are made up of a network of people. Each and every person then have a documentation of the whole history of all the transactions he has made as well as the balance of every account.

Let's have an example

A transaction would be a file indicating that person 1 gave a number of coins to person 2, then it is signed by the private key of person 1. Basically, it makes use of public key cryptography. After the transaction has been signed, it is then transmitted to all the other people in the network.

The whole network of people is then informed of the transaction but it is only confirmed after a specified amount of time. It would be good to note that confirmation is a vital part of cryptocurrency. In fact, you can say that cryptocurrency is all about confirmation.

You see, if the transaction isn't confirmed, it remains in a pending status, making it prone to being forged. As soon as a transaction has been confirmed, it is already permanent. It can't be forged, it cannot be undone and it has already been documented in the transaction record of the so-called blockchain.

This is where miners come in. The job of the miners is to confirm transactions in a network of cryptocurrencies, and only they are able to do this. What they do is they accept the transactions, verify them as legitimate then share them in the network. After a miner has confirmed a transaction, it has to be added to the database, therefore making it part of the blockchain.

As a reward for doing their job, miners are given tokens of the cryptocurrency as compensation. So you can see how valuable miners are to the whole concept of cryptocurrency.

Because of this, it would be relevant to take a more profound look at what miners are actually doing. Delve into the details of their work and how they keep cryptocurrencies going.

The fact is, anyone can be a miner. As the network is decentralized it has no power to assign tasks, so the cryptocurrency needs a kind of procedure to avoid a ruling party from misusing it. For instance, without this procedure, a person would be able to create a multitude of persons to scatter forged transaction, therefore destroying the system.

History Of Cryptocurrency

Cryptocurrency existed as a theoretical construct long before the first digital alternative currencies debuted. Early cryptocurrency proponents shared the goal of applying cutting-edge mathematical and computer science principles to solve what they perceived as practical and political shortcomings of "traditional" fiat currencies.

Technical Foundations

Cryptocurrency's technical foundation dates back to the early 1980s, when an American cryptographer named David Chaum invented a "blinding" algorithm that remains central to modern web-based encryption. The algorithm allowed for secure, unalterable information exchanges between parties, laying the groundwork for future electronic currency transfers. This was known as "blinded money."

By the late 1980s, Chaum enlisted a handful of other cryptocurrency enthusiasts in an attempt to commercialize the concept of blinded money. After relocating to the Netherlands, he founded DigiCash, a for-profit company that produced units of currency based on the blinding algorithm. Importantly, DigiCash's control wasn't decentralized, as is the case with Bitcoin and most other modern cryptocurrencies – DigiCash itself had a monopoly on supply control, similar to central banks' monopoly on fiat currencies.

DigiCash initially dealt directly with individuals, but the Netherlands' central bank cried foul and crashed this idea. Faced with an ultimatum, DigiCash agreed to sell only to licensed banks, seriously curtailing its market potential. Microsoft later approached DigiCash about a potentially lucrative partnership that would allow early Windows users to make purchases in its currency, but the two companies couldn't agree on terms, and DigiCash went belly-up in the late 1990s.

Around the same time, an accomplished software engineer named Wei Dai published a white paper on b-money, a virtual currency architecture that included many of the basic components of modern cryptocurrencies, such as complex anonymity protections and decentralization. However, b-money was never deployed as a means of exchange.

Shortly thereafter, a Chaum associate named Nick Szabo developed and released a cryptocurrency called Bit Gold, which was notable for using the block chain system that underpins most modern cryptocurrencies. However, Bit Gold never gained popular traction and is no longer used as a means of exchange.

Pre-Bitcoin Virtual Currencies

After DigiCash, much of the research and investment in electronic financial transactions shifted to more conventional, though digital, intermediaries, such as PayPal. A handful of DigiCash imitators, such as Russia's WebMoney, sprang up in other parts of the world.

In the United States, the most notable virtual currency of the late 1990s and 2000s was known as e-gold. e-gold was created and controlled by a Florida-based company of the same name. e-gold, the company, basically functioned as a digital gold buyer. Its customers, or users, sent their old jewelry, trinkets, and coins to e-gold's warehouse, receiving digital "e-gold" – units of currency denominated in ounces of gold. e-gold users could then trade their holdings with other users, cash out for physical gold, or exchange their e-gold for U.S. dollars.

At its peak in the mid-2000s, e-gold had millions of active accounts and processed billions of dollars in transactions annually. Unfortunately, e-gold's relatively lax security protocols made it a popular target for hackers and phishing scammers, leaving its users vulnerable to financial loss. And by the mid-2000s, much of e-gold's transaction activity was legally dubious – its laid-back legal compliance policies made it attractive to money laundering operations and small-scale Ponzi schemes. The platform faced growing legal pressure during the mid- and the late-2000s, and finally ceased to operate in 2009.

How to Get Started

If you have read through the information in the rest of the guidebook and you still feel like mining is the right choice for you, then you are ready for a great adventure. For the right person, mining can be a great way to challenge yourself, to learn more about the cryptocurrency market than anyone else can, and a good way to make some money.

Before you get into mining, you need to have a few items in place to help. You will find that joining with your regular computer, for example, is not the best way to earn a good profit with mining. You need a specialized computer, unless you want to never use your regular computer again, as well as a wallet to hold your coins, a good processor, and some motivation to get the work done. Let's look at some of the other things that you will need in order to get started with mining cryptocurrencies.

The hardware

The first thing we will look at is the hardware. To begin, you will need to get a mining hardware. When these currencies began, it was possible to use your own computer and a high-speed video processor card in order to mine.

But thanks to how popular these have gotten recently and how hard the equations are now, it is no longer possible to do this. When it comes to the mining industry, especially when we are talking about Bitcoin (BTC), you may need to use some customer Bitcoin ASIC chips because they offer performance that can be more than 100 times that of some older systems.

It is a good idea to get a good ASIC chip to help with your mining. Using an older system or missing out on this part means that you will use up more electricity than you would be able to earn.

Best mining services

Another option that you can use is to purchase a cloud mining contract. This is going to simplify the process, but it can increase the risk since you are not going to be the one who controls the physical hardware. Let's look at some of the most popular cloud mining services for Bitcoin that you may want to consider:

- Genesis Mining Review: Genesis is the largest Bitcoin provider and has expanded out to scrypt cloud mining as well. There are three plans for mining Bitcoin and it is priced reasonably for most people to start. They are also working to make Zcash mining contracts for users.

- Hashing 24 Review: This company has been working with Bitcoin mining since 2012, so it has some history to back it up. They use some modern ASIC chips to provide the best performance and efficiency that they can.

- Minex Review: Minex is an aggregator of blockchain projects that are presented in a game format. Users will be able to purchase Cloud packs that can be used to build up an index from a pre-picked set of cloud mining farms, real-world markets, casinos, and lotteries.

- Epbot Review: This is a good one to use if you need to save money while getting started. You can start with the cloud mining process for about $10, and you can break even pretty quickly.

Mining hardware

You also have to consider the type of hardware that you would like to use. There are a lot of options, but you need to balance out the cost and efficiency of the hardware with how much you can earn. The containers are a good option. AntMiner S7 can help you earn about 0.1645 BTC each month and will cost under $480 for the product while the AntMiner S9 can provide you with 0.3603 BTC on average each month for a cost under $2000. Another option is to go with the Avalon6 which will provide you with an average 0.1232 BTC each month for about $500.

It is often about picking the one that is the best price for how much you can earn. Most of the hardware is going to cost you a little bit so get ready to come up with this as your start-up cost.

You also need to make sure that you are picking out a good system that can help you to do the work. If you plan to do this on occasion and you are using one of the smaller cryptocurrencies, you may be able to get away with using your own personal computer. However, if you are serious about getting into mining, you need to consider a much better computer. Pick one that has good speed, has a good graphics card, and will be able to support the software that you need. This may cost a bit, but you do not want to go cheap on these or you will miss out on some great opportunities to earn money.

The software

If your head is reeling a bit from the costs in the past section, then this one is going to be a bit nicer. Once you have been able to choose the mining hardware that you want to use, it is time to download the mining software. Most mining software is going to be free to download, even that which is used to mine Bitcoin. There are quite a few options that you can make, so search around and find the one that can do the work the best. Two popular options that Bitcoin users like include BFGminer and CGminer, which are considered line programs.

If you would like to work with the GUI because it is easier to use, then EasyMiner can be a good option. This option is going to work out well with Android, Linux, and Windows programs so keep this in mind when you set it up.

Join a mining pool

There are some miners who choose to do all the work on their own. They spend a lot of money to get all the hardware and other things that they need, and then they do the work by themselves. This has the benefit of providing you with a bigger profit when you solve one of the codes. But with all the competition out there for competing for the codes, it is likely that, without joining a mining pool, you could spend a long time working on the codes and never making any profit.

It is often best to work in a mining pool. These pools allow you to make a good income in mining by working with others who share the same goal as you. You will receive one part of the mathematical equation to work on, and then others will work on the rest. Once you get a successful code, everyone who worked on the code will share in the profit.

This method provides you with a steadier source of income compared to doing it all on your own. It is much faster since you can work on it together with other people. You also won't have to use up as much power and electricity in your own home since everyone is sharing in. No, you won't get the full amount like you would when you do the work on your own, but you are more likely to get paid something when you work in a mining pool.

Set up your wallet

If you want to get paid after successfully completing the work of a miner, then you need to set up a wallet. There are many wallet options out there and it will often depend on the type of currency that you are working on for which one you will choose. There are some that are specific to just a few types of coins and others that can be used for a variety of ones. Make sure that you are picking out a wallet that is easy to use and known to be secure and safe. You do not want a hacker to get ahold of your wallet information and then steal all your coins while you are working.

When you sign up for a wallet, you will receive a unique address that is yours to use. If you can pick out your own address, make it something that no one else can link back to you to help with keeping your privacy. You can use this address to make sure that you get your coins when you are all done mining.

News resources

As a miner, it is important that you learn how to stay up to date with all the news regarding your digital currency of choice. This can help you to figure out if the coins are still a good one to go with or if you need to switch out because it is going to start losing value. There are a lot of different news sources that you can go, such as the WeUseCoins news section. Check up on this on a regular basis so you know what is going on with your currency always.

A dedicated spot to do the work

Some people find that so that to successfully mine, they need to set up a spot that is just for their mining equipment. If you are serious about doing the mining, then this is critical to help you see results. First, it is nice to have a computer that is just for the mining work that you do.

This makes it easier for your mining rig to run all the time and can increase your profits. You can use the same computer for mining and for personal use, but it can cause some hassles that you probably don't want to deal with.

In addition, you most likely want to pick out a place that is dark and can be kept cool. Your mining rig is going to make the computer run warm and if you leave the computer somewhere that it is already warm, you could run into issues with the computer overheating. Most people choose to leave their mining rig in the basement where it can stay nice and cold. You may also want to consider leaving a nice fan in the room as well to give the computer some extra protection.

Getting started with mining is serious business. It can take a lot of time and dedication and you will need to take the time to purchase various equipment if you want to see success in this endeavor. But when all the parts come together, you will be able to make a good profit with the help of mining.

How much is the amount of starting investment?

There is no small or large amount of investment that rather depends on how much you can afford. Don't think of how much exactly you invest, but rather what percentage of your funds you're going to invest into Bitcoins.

Before investing yourself, read articles and watch videos about cryptocurrency. Don't invest just because some people invest. Learn about crypto and make your own judgment then ask yourself: Do you believe Bitcoin will be successful? If yes, how likely? And then think of how much of your total money you should invest. DON'T invest more than you are willing to lose.

While there is not really starting amount you can say you want something substantial that will make something of a difference. Say, making $0.01 a day is nothing substantial but if you can make it $0.10 a day that's a good starting point of $3 a month. Then you grow, and sometimes you earn $30 a month or $1 per day so that you can make a decent investment and you carry on from there. Start small and get used to it.

Therefore, it totally depends on you, whatever amount you can manage or afford is the good amount of the investment. There is not a recommended amount since every person has their own circumstances. There are those that can only afford 0.001 BTC, whereas there are people that can afford several BTC as the starting investment.

More practically, if you are just a beginner, suggest starting with at least $50 to $100, which allows you to put 40% in Bitcoins and 4 to 6 alternative coins (Altcoins) so that you can achieve diversification on your portfolio. Even with small capital invested diversification is important to reduce your risk. The idea is to grow your savings and do so without taking too much risk.

The basic rule is that you shouldn't invest more than you can afford to lose. Don't forget cryptocurrency is a high-risk investment, so, as a rule of thumb, do not spend more than 10% of your net worth on it.

Advantages of Cryptocurrency

Modern Cryptocurrency Boom

WordPress was the first major company to accept payment in bitcoin in 2012. Then others like Microsoft, Expedia, and Newegg.com followed.

Advantages of Cryptocurrency

- Built-in scarcity: The source code of cryptocurrencies specifies how many units can ever exist. In this way, these electronic currencies are more like precious metals than common currencies because they are hardwired for scarcity. Like precious metals, cryptocurrency offers inflation protection, which is unavailable for paper currency users.

- Don't have government currency monopolies: Outside the direct control of national banks, such as the European Central Bank and U.S. Federal Reserve, cryptocurrencies offer a reliable means of exchange. This is particularly attractive for people who fear long-term economic instability because of the loose monetary policy of the government. Many political scientists and economists expect various governments to co-opt cryptocurrency or incorporate aspects of cryptocurrency (such as the authentication protocols and built-in scarcity) into common currencies.

- Self-Policing, Self-Interested communities: Mining is a built-in policing mechanism and quality control for cryptocurrencies. Minors are paid for their efforts. So they keep an up-to-date and accurate record. This secures the value of the currency and integrity of the system.

- Robust privacy protections: Anonymity and privacy were the chief concerns for early cryptocurrency advocates and still is. Many cryptocurrency users use aliases separate from any accounts, information, or stored data that could pinpoint them. It is possible for advanced community members to deduce the user's identities. Post-bitcoin or newer cryptocurrencies have additional protections that make it much more difficult.

- Out of government control: Governments can seize or freeze domestic bank accounts or converse financial transactions made in local countries. On the other hand, cryptocurrency is decentralized in nature and transaction records and funds are stored in various parts around the world, which prevents the attempt of state seizure.

- Usually cheaper than traditional electronic transactions: The wallets, private keys, and block keys effectively solve the double spending problem. Security ensures that newcomers in the cryptocurrency world aren't abused by experienced users who are capable of duplicating digital funds. Cryptocurrencies eliminate the need for a third-party, such as PayPal and Visa to verify and authenticate every electronic financial transition. So this eliminates the need for mandatory transaction fees. Cryptocurrency transition fees are usually less than 1% of the transition value. But PayPal and credit card takes 1.5% to 3%.

- Fewer barriers and costs to cross-border transitions: Unlike domestic transitions, cryptocurrencies don't treat international transitions differently than domestic transitions. Transactions either come with a normal transaction fee or are free. Regardless of where the money sender and money receiver are located. When compared with international transactions involving common currency, this is a huge advantage. International transitions always have an ATM or Credit Card fee.

How to Mine Cryptocurrency

Mining cryptocurrency is very much like a digital gold rush. First, you have to make an investment of a few hundred dollars in equipment and make a small profit. Then you have to put in months of mining time before the mandatory difficulty starts.

Feathercoins, dogecoins, and litecoins are there script-based cryptocurrencies that are best cost-benefit for beginners. For example, at the current value of litecoins, a person can earn anything from 50 cents to 10 dollars daily using consumer level mining hardware. Feathercoins and dogecoin will yield slightly less profit with the same mining hardware.

Is it worth it to mine Cryptocoins?

As a hobby, mining cryptocoins can be a really interesting adventure. Once starting, it will give you one or two dollars daily. Particularly, feathercoins, dogecoins, and litecoins are very accessible for regular people to mine. And if you invest $1000 in hardware, it will take about 18 to 24 months to get it back.

As a second income. In reality, cryptocoin or currency mining is a reliable source of income for most people. Only if you willing to invest $3000 to $5000 in up-front hardware costs, you can start to earn $50 daily or more. If you decide to try cryptocurrency mining, start as a hobby and a limited income. If you want to take it as a second income, then you should start to buy cryptocurrency instead of mining them.

How cryptocurrency mining works

The whole focus of mining is to accomplish three things:

- Mining is basically 24/7 computer accounting known as verifying transactions. So start by providing bookkeeping services to the coin network.

- Receive fractions of coins every couple of days as a payment for your accounting services.

- Keep your personal costs down, including hardware and electricity

Here is a list of what you need to start cryptocurrency mining:

- A coin wallet, which is basically a free private database. This password-protected wallet keeps a network-wide ledger of transactions and stores your earnings.

- A free mining software package made up of stratum and cgminer.

- You need a membership in an online cryptocurrency mining community. A mining community is a community of miners who join their computers to increase income stability and profitability.

- You need to join an online currency exchange. You will need it to exchange your conventional cash for virtual coins and vice versa.

- A high-speed, reliable internet connection. Preferably 2 megabits or faster speed.

- A hardware setup that is located in a cool spot, such as in your basement or an air-conditioned space.

- A custom-build or desktop computer designed for mining. You can start with your current computer, but while the miner is running you won't be able to use the computer. So you need a separate dedicated computer. Don't use a gaming console, handheld device, or a laptop for mining because these devices are not powerful enough to produce income.

- The costly matter: You need a dedicated processing device known as a mining ASIC chip or an ATI graphics processing card (GPU). For each new ASIC chip or GPU, the price is anywhere from $80 for used and $600 for new.

- A house fan to flow cooler air across your mining computer. Mining generates considerable heat, and cooling the hardware is critical for your success.

- Personal curiosity: You need to learn a lot about the topic. Cryptocurrency mining is an ongoing technology and you need to learn constantly. The very best cryptocurrency miners spend hours every week studying the best ways to adjust and improve.

Why you do not mine Bitcoins?

If you started earlier, for example, during 2009, you could have earned a lot of money by mining Bitcoin. But now Bitcoin mining is reserved for large companies only. During the past 5 years, the mathematical challenge of finding Bitcoins has become really difficult. Current up-front investment and another maintenance costs of mining are no longer worth it for home base operators. There is now no profit in mining Bitcoins unless you are willing to spend tens of thousands of dollars on an air-conditioning system and industrial hardware.

Things to Careful About when Mining Cryptocurrency

Just like any investment, there are risks involved with cryptocurrency investment. Because cryptocurrency is not regulated like conventional banking, you can't hope for an insurance when things go wrong. The risks that involve cryptocurrency mining:

- Losing your digital wallet of coins: You can lose your wallet several ways. For example, your online provider going out of business, your hard drive breaking down and you losing the wallet physically or forgetting your password.

- Deceitful mining pool organizers: Deceitful pool organizers could skim coins from you or take all your earnings all together and vanish.

- Electricity costs make your mining unprofitable: Electricity cost or hardware cost can make your mining campaign unprofitable.

- Hackers: a Talented hacker can break into your mining pool and steal coins from you and others.

- Feathercoins, dogecoin, litecoins all may drop in value.

Reduce your coin mining risks

There is no risk-free business, but you can certainly lower your cryptocurrency mining risk. Here are some suggestions:

- Losing your digital wallet of coins: Keeping a personal wallet on your home computer and keeping your password written down is a safe thing to do.

- Dishonest mining pool organizers: To avoid dishonest mining pool organizers, find a very active pool where the members are very active and keep constant eyes on pool organizers.

- Electricity costs: You can try various ways to lower your electricity cost.

- Hackers: The combination of personal habit and hardware is the best prevention against getting hacked. Place your coin wallet on a USB drive or on a detachable hard drive. Detach the hard drive when you are not using it. Backup your wallet regularly and transfer your currency from online to the detachable wallet.

Benefits and Risks of Investing

Benefits

Financial Self-Determinism and Control

The cryptocurrency networks are one of a kind because they are a digital store of value where people can securely save cryptocurrency units and enter into transactions without the need to rely on any third party regulatory body. After you have acquired and safely secured your cryptocurrency units, it is almost impossible for other people (thieves, hackers, banks or even the government) to take them away from you. The government cannot authorize the freezing of your cryptocurrency account nor stop you from entering into any transactions within the cryptocurrency network. This is the primary reason why people love cryptocurrencies because the lack of regulation allows free movement of money. The government can only do as much as track cryptocurrency purchases with fiat currencies but they cannot track purchases using cryptocurrencies by the individual.

Lower Cost of Transactions

While frozen accounts may be problematic, you also need to be aware of the cost of getting a transaction ready for use. On top of the unexpected risks of frozen accounts and massive chargebacks when you use payment processors, you will also be exposed to well-known high transaction charges for the services of these payment processors. This can considerably reduce the income of your business.

The transaction charges of PayPal, Google Checkout, and Amazon Checkout all begin at 2.9 percent plus $ 0.30 for each transaction. You can enjoy a lower rate of 1.9 percent only if your total transactions for the monthly amount to more than $ 30,000. Because of this, these exorbitant fees may burden a business with a low-profit margin. The same goes for businesses that require a lot of smaller transactions or those whose products are sold at a nominal price.

In contrast to current day transactions, cryptocurrencies are known for their low fees, a major reason why banks are looking to adopt them. The fees vary according to which cryptocurrency is being traded. Bitcoin is known for their high fees relative to other cryptocurrencies; however, Ethereum and Litecoin can have fees less than 1%. And then there is Ripple… It is basically free (not free but it's really cheap) to send Ripple tokens around. This is important because even though 1-2% may not seem like a lot, but when compounded interest is taken place over months, and years, this could equate to thousands, and even millions on large scale trading. This is true primarily for large banks where billions of dollars' worth of transactions is done annually! To put that into perspective, 2% of 1 billion dollars is $20 million! If you could invest that $20 million into somewhere and got a 10% return, that difference in fees is actually much more than 2%.

It Works Around the World

The cryptocurrency network is considered to be an intrinsically wide-reaching and global network. One of the biggest arguments for cryptocurrencies is the fast and low-cost transaction speeds across the world. You will not have to pass through artificial barriers to make payments to vendors who are based in other countries or regions. In fact, it is not entirely possible to validate where a particular cryptocurrency transaction originated. An online vendor who accepts cryptocurrency units as a mode of payment can instantly gain access to a global market while facing the risk of non-payment from customers who reside outside his own country and who are not bound by the legal system of his government. For example, this will allow individuals from the United States to send money to people in Australia in less than 10 minutes, making this much more convenient than third-party transactions which are costly. I tried sending money through Western Union and they charged me around 1.5% on top of a poor exchange rate. With cryptocurrencies, I can send some Litecoin in less than 5 minutes and it'll cost around 20 cents.

You should be aware of whether cryptocurrency use in your area is valid and viable for use. The legality of cryptocurrencies will vary based on the country you get your transaction in. In 2017, the cryptocurrency world saw a larger adoption in cryptocurrency use and cryptocurrency technology. In fact, more Bitcoin ATMs are available, allowing withdrawal of Bitcoin to cash, as well as, more vendors accepting Bitcoin and other cryptocurrencies as a form of payments. These signs show the availability and potential of cryptocurrencies. That being said, there are also countries that are closing off cryptocurrencies.

Risks

Volatility of Cryptocurrency Prices

When someone asks you what the value of the cryptocurrency units that you own is, how can you readily answer the question? The fundamental value of any particular currency is a function of the consumer demand for that currency and the consumers' capability to use the currency to trade it for valuable goods and services. Because a lot of conventional currencies are no longer linked to the worth of an underlying product or commodity such as gold and other precious metals, a cryptocurrency unit will only be valuable when some people or consumers want to own them and use them for trade. So if one day the world decides there is no longer a need for cryptocurrencies, the prices will plummet. Though this is unlikely, it is still a potential risk.

Currently, there are plenty (approximately 7000) of public exchanges that have been set up to allow consumers to buy and sell cryptocurrency units in exchange for dollars or other common currencies. This aids in establishing a fundamental relative value for cryptocurrencies, which then allow vendors to convert their cryptocurrency holdings into other common currencies on a more regular basis. This minimizes the vendors' risk exposure to the price volatility of cryptocurrencies. As more individuals trade cryptocurrencies, the likely hood of cryptocurrencies to become more adopted increases.

Even though during the recent years, the price of cryptocurrencies has significantly fluctuated, there now exist methods that vendors can use to quote cryptocurrency prices relative to their equivalent value in dollar or other common currency. This also allows them to convert the cryptocurrencies they have collected into another currency immediately. A common database for cryptocurrency prices is www.coinmarketcap.com, which shows all cryptocurrencies available on the market, all historical prices, all exchanges with everything you need to know.

This comparatively small market limitation together with the absence of a regulatory body may expose the prices of cryptocurrencies to become manipulated by the market players. It's like what you would expect out of penny stocks and other items that are not as commonplace; it only takes one or two transactions for the values of certain items to be jacked up and artificially influenced. In the past, when there has been positive news, or speculation, some institutions (even countries) can jack up the prices. This has been seen frequently with the Korean market, jacking up various cryptocurrencies such as Ethereum, Ripple, and Litecoin (amongst many), resulting in periods where 50% of trade occurs solely in the Korean market.

Several important speculations are being made in various online forums on who may be behind the price manipulation of cryptocurrencies and to what extent. It is quite common to hear cryptocurrency speculators refer to "The Manipulator" when they discuss significant market movements.

"The Manipulator" refers to an unidentified individual or group of people that are assumed to be controlling the cryptocurrency prices through their vast wealth. But it is not clear as to who these people are.

There are various social media channels and networks such as Facebook groups, Youtube channels and other sites such as Reddit, that contain a lot of hype by individuals with extensive influence. Keep in mind, even though they might have a rational reason for their 'hyping' of a specified coin, this could also be considered as market manipulation. My advice is not to take my advice, but also do your own research. There are plenty of individuals that are invested in specific coins that only want to make money. Know what you're investing in. Period.

One thing is for certain that the relatively anonymous nature of cryptocurrencies is a huge part of what allows people to adjust the values of cryptocurrencies as they see fit. This makes for an added risk to the cryptocurrency. Of course, whoever is regulating it could always stop doing so and focus on some other kind of investment in the future, but it can be near impossible to figure out what's going to happen.

Risk of Loss

When you own cryptocurrency units, it is quite apparent that you have the responsibility to ensure that your digital wallet is secured from any potential hazards of loss and theft. This task or responsibility can be quite taxing, especially if you own a substantial number of cryptocurrencies because you will have to use certain tools such as protected encryption, password management, and information backup to make sure that your risks are maintained at a low-level.

Several high-profile incidents have already been reported where people made errors and mistakes in handling their cryptocurrency accounts that ultimately led to them losing a large amount of their cryptocurrencies. Since there is no central authority you can approach to seek help or assistance, you may have to completely write off your losses because they may already be unrecoverable.

The risks associated with cryptocurrencies are critical and have to be identified. It should not be a surprise that a virtual currency that is relatively new is in danger of being hacked into. You should be cautious when seeing how this currency is run before you make any trades with it.

Few things to consider…

- Although it may seem common sense, NEVER hand out your private keys to anyone. The private keys given by any wallet is the code that allows direct access to your cryptocurrencies.
- Consider a hardware device. Keeping your funds offline can be added protection, however, the risk of losing your hard-wallet is likely.
- Never leave funds on exchanges. If you've been in the cryptocurrency world for a while, you would know several major hacks in the past that have resulted in multi-million dollar loses. Most notably the Mt. Gox hack.

Additionally, leaving your cryptocurrencies on exchanges leaves your funds subject to the exchanges' rules. A good example is an incident on 1st August 2017, with the introduction of Bitcoin Cash. Any Bitcoin owned on Coinbase is subject to Coinbase terms and conditions. Coinbase chose not to give any Bitcoin Cash to any Bitcoin owners during the Bitcoin hardfork. Exchanges are not liable for any loss that has occurred, so protect yourself.

Regulatory Ambiguity

The legal category of cryptocurrencies remains uncertain. Some people consider it as a commodity like gold and silver while others treat it as a viable currency. Still, there are others who look at them as a financial product or something that is legally equal to the gold in World of Warcraft. It is yet to be known if they will someday require licenses and financial rules and regulations for it to become a truly viable currency.

Mt.Gox, which was considered as the biggest Bitcoin exchange market, has reported that they have experienced some difficulties in wiring funds. This is because of certain money laundering investigations are done by the government or regulatory agencies.

But cryptocurrencies are intrinsically difficult to regulate because no central authority oversees all transactions. Because of this, it is highly probable that cryptocurrencies can become the primary medium option for people who are into illicit activities such as money laundering and tax evasion.

What makes the cryptocurrency market such a concern is that the protected nature of the currency makes it popular among those who engage in illegal or questionable activities.

But if we stop and think about it, any paper currency such as the US dollar can also have the same risks as described above. It is also possible to complete illegal transactions anonymously using dollar bills because it is possible to exchange it without any auditable paper trails. But the complexity of the cryptocurrency network technology may instigate regulators to see it as a hazard to the rules of law.

Cryptocurrency Exchanges

Before you start investing in cryptocurrencies, it would be wise to understand how exchanges work and what particular platforms you can work with.

Cryptocurrency Exchanges: What are They Really?

As cryptocurrencies are digital currencies, the exchanges where they are traded in are digital platforms, websites, which offer transactions like buying, selling, or trading. A cryptocurrency exchange works pretty much like a traditional stock or Forex exchange system. Professional brokers are accessible, self-trading is possible, and there are tools available to help you maximize each transaction.

Since transactions are coursed on the Web, these exchange platforms need to verify the identities of their participants. Just like social media accounts, email accounts, and such, you also need to create a user account on your platform of choice. You will then have to verify this account by providing the site with a valid identification card.

Although most exchanges require that participants have verified accounts, you will find others that are not too strict. The commonality between these exchanges is that they can accommodate self-made, straightforward trades.

The Different Kinds of Cryptocurrency Exchanges

There are different kinds of cryptocurrencies and there are also varying exchanges available to those who have investments or want to trade these digital assets. To start you off, here are the three primary exchanges that you can consider if you want to take part in the world of cryptocurrencies.

1. Brokers

What you have with brokers are websites that exist for the sole purpose of selling cryptocurrencies. It is the broker site that sets the price. A cryptocurrency broker is comparable to an outlet that offers foreign exchange services.

2. Trading Platforms

The trading platforms for cryptocurrencies work by connecting buyers and sellers in one place. The sites earn their income by taking a certain percentage off from every transaction done in the portal. You can say that this is their service fee. Trading platforms are excellent channels for simple, straightforward trading.

3. Direct Trading Systems

Direct trading systems are different from your everyday cryptocurrency trading platforms because they can accommodate more complex trades within the platform. Aside from just being a place for buying or selling cryptocurrencies, participants can actually engage in dynamic exchanges within the system.

In addition, the platform does not only offer buying or selling but constant trading amongst investors around the world. Unlike standard platforms, traders are not bound by set market prices for their cryptocurrencies. They can actually set their own prices for these digital assets. It is now in the discretion of the other investors if they want to proceed with an exchange or not.

As you can see, the types of exchanges for cryptocurrency vary from basic to complex. As an investor, you can expect yourself to go through all of these channels as you engage in the trade.

What Should You Look for in a Cryptocurrency Exchange?

Just like with other investment channels, it is important that you do not simply go with the first option that you see. In this case, you will be dealing with digital assets that carry real monetary values. This is why you should not leave anything to chance. Before you even consider buying cryptocurrencies to trade with, you should do some research as there are different exchanges available online.

If you do not know where to begin, here are some guidelines that may hopefully help in your search for the most suitable exchange.

- Credibility

Credibility is essential when it comes to cryptocurrency trading. You do not want to lose your investment or experience unnecessary problems just because you did not check your chosen exchange out.

You have the Internet on your side, use it to your benefit. Aside from checking the platform itself, search for relevant reviews from people who have actually used the platform with success. Asking for referrals is another excellent option. Also, there are trustworthy industry websites that can be consulted as well. If you need more assistance, you can even participate in forums.

- Registration Process and Requirements

Simplicity is the name of the game when it comes to account creation. You want to create a trading account in a few minutes and successfully verify it in an equally short amount of time. Especially since you are working in the digital space, your chosen exchange should be optimized enough to have an efficient integrated registration system.

If your exchange cannot even perfect the registration process, just think of how problematic the platform may be when it comes to the actual transaction interface. Having practical verification processes is also important. Most of the time, exchanges that are not able to quickly verify accounts do not have the right technology for that purpose. In this case, chances are they will not also have the right technologies for the service or security.

- Verification and Security

Although verification is important, it should not be excessive or unrealistic in terms of identification requirements. Usually, a government-issued ID card will be enough to allow you to deposit or withdraw money from your account. Verification may take anywhere from a few minutes to several days but it ensures that your account and transactions are always secure.

You will find exchanges that will permit you to transact in the system anonymously. These are the exchanges that you should watch out for. Usually, they offer minimal security or encryption that can easily jeopardize your transactions, not to mention your trading account on the platform. It would be best if you went through with the whole verification process for something like this. Protect yourself from hackers and scams.

- Geographical Conditions or Restrictions

Just like how Forex trading is regulated, the same applies to cryptocurrencies. As a result, site functionalities may differ from one location to another. There may be some tools that you can access in one country and not in another. This is why you should find an exchange that is fully-compatible given your country's geographical regulations.

- Exchange Rates

When it comes to exchange rates, these actually differ from one platform to another. This is why you should practice the concept of "shopping around" when you search for cryptocurrency exchanges. There are times when an exchange would have rates that are significantly lower than the market rate. You may also be lucky enough to find high exchange rates that will work in your favor. So spend time comparing rates and services so that you can land the best deal on a secure exchange platform.

- Transaction and Service Fees

What you have here are pieces of information that should not be kept hidden by exchanges. It is necessary for them to publish these service and transaction rates in the site and you should definitely look for them when you pay the page a visit.

These fees tend to differ depending on the exchange. They are usually dependent on the extent of services that your membership comes with. If you are in a simple buying and selling exchange platform, you can expect lower rates compared to those that offer consistent trading.

In this case, the concept of "better service higher rates" does not always apply. This is why you should not base your decision simply on this component. What you have to set your mind to is finding a credible exchange that meets your needs and offers its services at a reasonable rate.

• Payment Methods and Processes

Keep in mind that cryptocurrencies involve real money. This is why you need to think about how you can pay and get paid should you decide to invest in these digital assets. When you assess potential exchanges to consider, find information with regard to the payment methods as well.

There are exchanges that offer credit or debit card transactions. Some may involve direct bank deposits. You will find others that patronize wire transfers while there are others that are more efficient as they leverage digital payment services like PayPal.

It is important that you find an exchange that can accommodate as many payment options as possible. Remember that you will be transacting with other people on the platform and you never know which method it is that they have access to. The more payment methods are accommodated by the platform, the more convenient it will be for you to transact in that system.

Aside from convenience, payment options also dictate transaction speeds. For example, credit card transactions are secure yet easier to verify and because of this, transactions are processed in minutes. As for wire transfers, on the other hand, these require manual processing by banks and may take several days, sometimes even weeks to complete.

Cryptocurrency Exchanges to Consider

As cryptocurrencies rose in popularity over the years, plenty of exchanges have popped up online. This makes it even more challenging, especially for beginners, to find the right platform to start with. To assist you in your search, here are some of the best exchanges that are worth your consideration.

It is suggested that you start with these so that you can easily get the hang of cryptocurrency investing. Here you have exchanges that actual users have rated to be top notch. You will also find those which have been rated based on their accessibility and functionality. And then there are those that trump the rest when it comes to security and transaction fees.

1. Gemini

It is primarily serving the purpose of trading Ether and Bitcoin cryptocurrencies. It is a highly-secure exchange platform. It offers a user-friendly interface and has regulated standards not to mention capital requirements. It functions closely like an actual bank and is highly liquid ensuring that you will get paid. Here, you can trade both cryptocurrency types with US dollars and vice versa.

2. Coinbase

Millions of traders are currently using Coinbase, making it one of the most popular exchanges available today. Aside from beginners, well-known traders are also taking part in the cryptocurrency game through this platform. The edge of Coinbase is that it offers a wide variety of tools and services yet is user-friendly. The transactions are secured and it even offers a built-in storage for your cryptocurrencies.

3. Bitstamp

With Bitstamp, you have one of the earliest trading platforms made available for Bitcoin. User-friendly yet highly-secure, it also offers Bitcoin storage within the platform. The best thing about the latter is that all stored Bitcoins are insured. User support is available all day every day. You can create a free account and begin participating in the trade. It is very easy and efficient to use.

4. Cexio

With Cexio, you have a universal cryptocurrency exchange platform. You can easily conduct trades here exchanging actual money for cryptocurrencies and vice versa. It is ideal for both newbies and experienced traders. Armed with user-friendly tools and functions, it is a great platform to start with. Also, the advantage you gain by using Cexio is with regard to its prices which closely reflect those of the markets.

5. Poloniex

Security is extremely important in the cryptocurrency game and this is something that can be expected from Poloniex, as an exchange platform. It supports hundreds of different cryptocurrencies and trading pairs, and offers a series of tools both for novices and advanced investors alike. The beauty of this platform is that you can always expect to close a position.

6. Kraken

If your chosen cryptocurrency is the Bitcoin, then Kraken would be an ideal exchange option. It is one of the largest Bitcoin trading platforms available today. It is even a partner of the primary digital bank for cryptocurrencies. Although it is mainly used to trade Bitcoins, it can also accommodate Ether transactions and those involving other cryptocurrencies. It is the exchange of choice for traders who have more experience in the industry.

7. Shapeshift

As what was previously mentioned, there are certain exchanges that allow for anonymous trades. In this case, you can easily make straightforward trades without registering for an account with the help of Shapeshift. This will be an ideal exchange to use if you plan on making transactions using nothing else but cryptocurrencies.

List of Cryptocurrencies

Cryptocurrency usage has exploded since Bitcoin's release. Though exact active currency numbers fluctuate and individual currencies' values are highly volatile, the overall market value of all active cryptocurrencies is generally trending upward. At any given time, hundreds of cryptocurrencies trade actively.

The cryptocurrencies described here are marked by stable adoption, robust user activity, and relatively high market capitalization (greater than $10 million, in most cases):

1. Bitcoin

Bitcoin is the world's most widely used cryptocurrency, and is generally credited with bringing the movement into the mainstream. Its market cap and individual unit value consistently dwarf (by a factor of 10 or more) that of the next most popular cryptocurrency. Bitcoin has a programmed supply limit of 21 million Bitcoin.

Bitcoin is increasingly viewed as a legitimate means of exchange. Many well-known companies accept Bitcoin payments, though most partner with an exchange to convert Bitcoin into U.S. dollars before receiving their funds.

2. Litecoin

Released in 2011, Litecoin uses the same basic structure as Bitcoin. Key differences include a higher programmed supply limit (84 million units) and a shorter target block chain creation time (two-and-a-half minutes). The encryption algorithm is slightly different as well. Litecoin is usually the second- or third-most popular cryptocurrency by market capitalization.

3. Ripple

Released in 2012, Ripple is noted for a "consensus ledger" system that dramatically speeds up transaction confirmation and block chain creation times – there's no formal target time, but the average is every few seconds. Ripple is also more easily converted than other cryptocurrencies, with an in-house currency exchange that can convert Ripple units into U.S. dollars, yen, euros, and other common currencies.

However, critics have noted that Ripple's network and code are more susceptible to manipulation by sophisticated hackers and may not offer the same anonymity protections as Bitcoin-derived cryptocurrencies.

4. Ethereum

Launched in 2015, Ethereum makes some noteworthy improvements on Bitcoin's basic architecture. In particular, it utilizes "smart contracts" that enforce the performance of a given transaction, compel parties not to renege on their agreements, and contain mechanisms for refunds should one party violate the agreement. Though "smart contracts" represent an important move toward addressing the lack of chargebacks and refunds in cryptocurrencies, it remains to be seen whether they're enough to solve the problem completely.

5. Dogecoin

Dogecoin, denoted by its immediately recognizable Shiba Inu mascot, is a variation on Litecoin. It has a shorter block chain creation time (one minute) and a vastly greater number of coins in circulation – the creators' target of 100 billion units mined by July 2015 was met, and there's a supply limit of 5.2 billion units mined every year thereafter, with no known supply limit. Dogecoin is thus notable as an experiment in "inflationary cryptocurrency," and experts are watching it closely to see how its long-term value trajectory differs from that of other cryptocurrencies.

6. Coinye

Coinye was developed under the original moniker "Coinye West" in 2013, and identified by an unmistakable likeness of hip-hop superstar Kanye West. Shortly before Coinye's release, in early 2014, West's legal team caught wind of the currency's existence and sent its creators a cease-and-desist letter.

To avoid legal action, the creators dropped "West" from the name, changed the logo to a "half man, half fish hybrid" that resembles West (a biting reference to a "South Park" episode that pokes fun at West's massive ego), and released Coinye as planned. Given the hype and ironic humor around its release, the currency attracted a cult following among cryptocurrency enthusiasts. Undaunted, West's legal team filed suit, compelling the creators to sell their holdings and shut down Coinye's website.

Though Coinye's peer-to-peer network remains active and it's still technically possible to mine the currency, person-to-person transfers and mining activity have collapsed to the point that Coinye is basically worthless.

Blockchain Technology

The Blockchain is a clever and original invention of Satoshi Nakamoto – a pseudonym of a person or a group of people. But since its inception, it has grown to something more, and one of the biggest questions that people ask is: what exactly is blockchain?

By letting digital information be shared, but not replicated, blockchain made the internet a new backbone. It was originally created for Bitcoin, a digital currency, but the tech community had found other possible uses for this technology.

A lot of people refer to Bitcoin as 'digital gold,' and probably for a good reason. So far, the market capitalization of Bitcoin is nearing 200 billion USD. Blockchains are also able to create other digital value. Just like with your car or the internet, you don't have to learn how the blockchain works in order to use it. However, it doesn't hurt to have a basic understanding of this technology. By knowing the basics of this technology, you will understand why it is considered significant and revolutionary.

Distributed Database

Imagine a spreadsheet duplicated over a thousand times throughout a computer network. Then visualize that the network was made to update the spreadsheet regularly. That's blockchain. Basic, right?

Blockchain houses information that exists as a shared database. There is no centralized form of the information that a hacker can corrupt. Anybody on the internet can access the data because it is hosted by millions of computers at the same time.

Like the internet, blockchain is built with robustness. Since there are stored blocks of identical information all throughout the network, no single person can control the blockchain and there is no single failure point.

Bitcoin was created in 2008, and since then the Bitcoin blockchain has worked without any major disruptions. The problems that have occurred with Bitcoin are because of mismanagement or hacking. Basically, the problems came from human errors and bad intention, not from flaws in its concepts. The internet has been durable for nearly 30 years. That's an achievement that bodes well for the continuous development of blockchain.

Being in a constant state of consensus, blockchain continuously checks itself every 10 minutes. The blockchain network reconciles each transaction in 10-minute interludes. Every transaction group is called a block. There are two properties that come from this:

    1. Transparency. The data is public because the data is inserted in the network as a whole.

    2. It is not able to be corrupted. A huge amount of computing power is needed to change any information in the blockchain to supersede the complete network.

We can conclude that it may be possible, but in actual practice, it's not very likely. If you control the system to get Bitcoins, it would also end up destroying their value.

Made Up of Nodes

There are networks of computing nodes that make up the blockchain. Together these nodes make a robust second-level network, a completely different way for the internet to work.

Each node works as an administrator for the blockchain. Each can join the network voluntarily; this makes the network decentralized. However, every one of them has an incentive for network participation: the possibility of getting Bitcoins.

Many believe that nodes mine Bitcoin, but this is a misnomer. In actuality, every one of them is competing to try and get Bitcoins by solving complex computations puzzles. Bitcoin was the main reason why blockchain was created. Or so that's what it seemed. Turns out, Bitcoin is only the first of the several different technology applications.

There are around 700 cryptocurrencies that are currently available. There are also other possible modifications of the original blockchain that are in development or currently active.

Decentralization

Blockchain was designed to be a decentralized technology. That means anything that will happen on the blockchain will be a function of the network in its entirety. Several important implications come from this. Through coming up with a new method in verifying the transactions, some aspects of traditional commerce may now be unnecessary.

Stock market trades can become nearly synchronous on the blockchain. It can also make record keeping, such as land registry, completely public. Decentralization is already a part of it.

A global computer network jointly controls the database that houses all of Bitcoin's transactions using this technology. This means that Bitcoin is controlled by its own network – not by a single authority. Since the network is decentralized, it operates on a peer-to-peer (P2P) basis. The different forms of mass collaboration that make this possible are only now beginning to be looked at.

You don't need complex knowledge about blockchain to use it. Currently, finance is one of the strongest uses for blockchain. The blockchain can possibly remove the mediators for a lot of transactions. The public got access to personal computing with the creation of GUI, graphical user interface, which turned into a 'desktop.' The most common GUI that was created for blockchain is the 'wallet' applications. They can be used to purchase online items with Bitcoin. They can also be used to store Bitcoins as well as other digital currencies.

Sharing Economy

With businesses like Airbnb and Uber growing, there is no doubt that the sharing economy has proven successful. Presently, users that are in need of a ride have to depend on services such as Uber. By using peer-to-peer payments, blockchain provides direct and effective transaction between parties.

A good example of this is OpenBazaar. They use blockchain to make a peer-to-peer version of eBay. If you download the app onto a computing device, you will be able to transact with OpenBazaar vendors without having to pay a transaction fee.

The fact that it doesn't have any rules means that the reputation of the participants will be more essential to the business interactions than with eBay.

Governance

With results becoming publicly accessible and transparent, elections or other poll taking events can become completely transparent because of the distributed database technology. The Ethereum-based smart contracts would help to automate this process. Boardroom, an app, enables making decisions to take place on a blockchain. This means that company governance could become completely verifiable and transparent when handling information, digital assets, or equity.

File Storage

There are plenty of benefits when it comes to making file storage decentralized. When you share data across the network, it helps to protect the files from being lost or hacked. InterPlanetary File System (IPFS) makes it easy to see the way a distributed web could operate.

Some other uses of blockchain include:

- Intellectual property protection
- Internet of Things
- Identity management

- Data management
- Land title registration
- Stock trading

What is an ICOs and how does it work

An ICO, or initial coin offering, is an unregulated way to raise funds for a new cryptocurrency. An ICO is typically used by startups to work around the regulated and rigorous capital-raising process that banks or venture capitalists require. With an ICO campaign, part of the cryptocurrency will be sold to the backers in exchange for other cryptocurrencies or legal tender.

Whenever startups are interested in raising money with an ICO, they will typically create whitepaper plan that states what their project is about, what they will, how much money they need to start, how many tokens the creators will keep for themselves, what money they will accept, and how long they will run their campaign. During their campaign, the supporters and enthusiast for their initiative will purchase some of their cryptocoins with virtual currency or fiat currency.

The coins they purchases are called tokens and are similar to company shares that are sold to investors during an IPO transaction. If they don't raise the minimum amount of money needed, the money that was invested is returned to the backers, and they deem the ICO unsuccessful. If they do meet the need funds, the money they raised will be used to initiate the scheme or finish it.

The investors in these ICOs are typically motivated to purchase the coin hoping that the plan will succeed once it launches, which may translate into a higher coin value than what they initially bought it for. One successful ICO that turned out to be profitable for the investors is Ethereum. Ethereum announced their project in 2014, and their ICO raised $0.40 per Ether or $18 million Bitcoins. Their project went live, officially, in 2015 and their ether value hit $14 in 2016 with a market cap of more than $1 billion.

Even though you can find successful ICO transactions, and they are typically poised to be a disruptive, innovative tool, investors need to be cautious as some crowdsale campaigns or ICOs are fraudulent. Since financial authorities don't regulate these fundraising operatives, like the SEC, funds that you lose through fraudulent initiatives probably won't be recovered.

The People's Bank of China, in early September 2017, banned ICOs. They stated the reason was that it was disruptive to financial and economic stability. The bank stated that the tokens could not be used for currency and banks were not able to provide services to ICOs. Because of this, Ethereum and Bitcoin tumbled, and they saw this as a sign that cryptocurrency regulations were on the way. Their ban also penalized offerings that had already been completed.

Now that you understand what ICOs are let's look five of the biggest ICO tokens.

NXT

NXT has a 1,477,000% ROI. NXT is one of the longest blockchain projects that are on the market. BCNext, an anonymous developer, launched NXT in November 2013, during a time when blockchain was still in its early stages and was pretty much unknown to the general public.

NXT held their ICO on BitcoinTalk Forum in September 2013. It was able to raise $16,800 worth of Bitcoins to create their new open source platform that used their proof-of-stake consensus mechanism for their currency, also known as NXT.

NXT was made for applications and financial services. They have their own marketplace, asset exchange, and message system. It also enables anyone like corporations, small business, and banks to create their own application.

In September 2013, NXT was worth $0.0000168 and in December 2017, it was worth $0.249.

IOTA

IOTA has a 332,500% ROI. By combining the Internet of Things and parts of blockchain technology, IOTA is looking to develop a transactional IoT settlement layer.

IOTA is the only big digital currency that doesn't make use of a complete blockchain to do their transactions. IOTA, instead, uses what they call a Tangle, which fixes the transaction fee and scalability issues that digital currencies face, like Bitcoin requiring the fund sender to conduct verification at the same time they send funds. The makes the entire ledger decentralized and makes a zero-fee transaction system because there are no fees that have to be paid to the participants.

In November and December of 2015, IOTA held their ICO, and they raised $400,000. IOTA tokens, during their crowdsale, were sold for less than $0.001, and every single one of the one billion tokens was sold.

On June 13, 2017, IOTA (MIOTA) started trading on exchanges at $0.63. In December 2017, the value of IOTA was at $1.43.

Ethereum

Ethereum has 152,500% ROI. Ethereum is an open-source and public distributed ledger that lets people create decentralized applications and smart contracts. Vitalik Buterin launched the project in 2013, and it has become one of the largest blockchain projects.

Their smart contracts platform has gained a lot of attention from lots of different industries because it could be useful in streamline and digitizing inefficient business processes. That's why their currency, ether, has seen a use increase in value.

They had their ICO in mid-2014, where 11.9 million tokens were sold and raised $16 million. Its price during their crowdsale came to $0.311. Ethereum carries the ticker ETH, and, in terms of market cap, it is the second largest digital currency. The all-time high of ether was $519.86, which it hit on November 29,2017. In December of 2017, it was at $472.50.

NEO

NEO has an ROI of 114,000%. NEO was rebranded from AntShares. It is a Chinese startup that is looking to develop a blockchain for digital asset ownership. They want to make a blockchain that works as a legal proof-of ownership that the broader society will accept. They have gained a lot of attention by combining digital assets and smart contracts to make a "smart assets platform."

In October 2015, NEO had their first ICO where they sold 17.5 million tokens and made $550,000. This was a time when

ICOs were still a fairly new phenomenon in the digital assets market. They launched at a price of $0.032 in 2015. They had a second crowdsale in September 2016 to further finance its platform. During this second offering, they sold 22.5 million tokens and raised $4.5 million. In December 2017 NEO was worth $36.20.

Stratis

Stratis has an 81,000% ROI. The Stratis startup provides users with a blockchain-as-a-service platform that is aimed at financial institutions that are looking to make solutions with the blockchain technology. The UK-based company has created a platform known as Stratis that lets enterprises to create a customized blockchain app and make private blockchains with the Stratis' blockchain.

Since their tools are mainly targeted at Microsoft products, Microsoft added their blockchain-as-a-Service to their cloud service. In June 2016, when Startis started is ICO, they raised $600,000 worth of currency.

Its issue price started at $0.007, and in December 2017 it was trading for $5.90. They reached an all-time high on June 5, 2017, for $11.47.

Successful Investment Strategies

Trading cryptocurrency gives you a short- and long-term financial freedom thus allowing not waste your time at pointless work, have a budget breakdown of costs to travel the world, and spend quality time with your family. Here are several sample newbies-friendly strategies that make this feasible. Upon acquiring experience, you can build and add your own strategies, some varying drastically and others minimally.

There are typically two types of crypto strategy:

- Investment –focusing more on macro crypto economics and asset fundamentals

- Trading – focusing more on market cycles and technical analysis

Investors typically tend to focus more on fundamental analysis with technical analysis used to support entry positions and portfolio balancing. Investing long-term enables you to benefit from the compound growth of both your portfolio and individual investments, enhancing this by diversifying profits from good investments into new opportunities. Where investing in stocks allows you to benefit from incremental income from dividends, with certain crypto investments you can do similar by staking and receiving newly minted coins from block rewards.

Traders typically tend to enter in and out of assets more regularly, using technical analysis to identify opportunities to buy in low on an asset and trade out either partial or full positions when reaching specific targets. Trading requires a high level of technical analysis and discipline, utilizing stop losses to limit losses on a bad trade.

It is very important to decide what kind of strategy is most suitable for you. One of the most important things is that too many people try and become traders when they should really just be investors.

Being a crypto investor, prefer to focus your time and energy on researching and understanding the macro crypto economy and investing in those assets which would exist over a more extended time-frame. As the inevitable market squeeze happens, you would your investments to be those that survive, similar to those who were invested in Google and Amazon when the dot-com bubble burst.

Tend, therefore, to focus your investments on the leading market cap assets, with a product in the market and not overvalued. You will though support these with speculative investments in disruptive crypto assets which may deliver significant multiple returns.

While you may on the rare occasion make short-term trades, this is usually in response to specific and obvious opportunities to make quick returns, either when the market or an asset is particularly undervalued, usually in response to a specific market movement.

In developing your strategy, consider this is a new highly speculative asset class so that investing in cryptocurrency is a bet on:

1. The acceptance, integration and normalization of virtual currencies as a store of value and medium of exchange alongside traditional fiat currencies.

2. The successful deployment of decentralized blockchain technology applications which achieve scale and thus economic viability.

Some of the fundamental investment hints are as follows:

− Aiming at the long-term goal, be able to sell crypto incrementally to fund your life.

− Aiming at increasing the size of your Bitcoin position.

− Aiming at increasing the size of other key trading pairs, which will exist after a crash and perform better than or similar to Bitcoin. Therefore, Bitcoin is a portfolio tier on its own. Other trading pairs are an individual tier too.

− Consider other investments to be split across new categories and traded to grow tier 1 and 2 positions.

− Aiming at tracking altcoins against both dollar and BTC value.

− Support your investments with incremental income from mining and staking.

More specifically, if you invest in Bitcoin, split your investments into specific tiers that may seem like

(i) Bitcoin;

(ii) Ethereum, Dash, and Monero as trading pairs;

(iii) Verge, ZCoin, and Dogecoin as currencies;

(iv) EOS, 0x, and Komodo as protocols;

(v) BAT, Civic, and Metal as utility tokens;

(vi) PoSW, NEBL, and Hush as micro-caps.

You can particularly focus on privacy coins, low cap protocols, Blockchain 3.0 protocols, masternodes, trustless staking, atomic swaps, decentralized exchanges, lightning network, zero fee coins.

Aiming at the growing of trading pairs, the investment strategy may seem like

(i) **Bitcoin long-term hold:** keep about 20% of your portfolio in Bitcoin, selling it off when Bitcoin scaling flippens;

(ii) **Bitcoin versus altcoin balancing:** balance that with respect to Bitcoin market trends, which can be found at https://coinmarketcap.com/charts/. Say, if Bitcoin market dominance is about 50% but falling (rising), your Bitcoin position may be kept at less (more) than 40% (60%);

(iii) **invest in altcoins to grow your** Bitcoin **position:** as altcoins are traded on most exchanges using the Bitcoin pair, sell them for more Bitcoin than you have paid. Trace the altcoin positions regularly trying to catch their peaks during a trading cycle aiming to complete the altcoin exit most closely to the peak benchmark;

(iv) **manage** tolerance for risk **on a daily basis, maintaining a cash float between 0 and 50%**. Basically, this takes your money off the table when waiting for a crash to happen.

(v) **rebalance your** Bitcoin **and primary trading pairs** when capturing a spike in asset values.

(vi) **choose your investments wisely** weighing in on the market gain and growth.

Rebalancing is the process of buying and selling portions of your portfolio in order to set the weight of each asset class back to its original state. When rebalancing your portfolio, move into new investments based on a combination of factors such as price, market capitalization charts, and general gut feel. Say, if a coin value is setting to make a parabolic move and you can interpret this as indicating overbought conditions, sell off some coins and move into another one. Alternatively, if the oversold conditions are met, increase your holding.

Cryptocurrency Mistakes And How To Avoid Them

Here a list of common mistakes people make. This is not an exhaustive list, so be sure you are always careful and do your due diligence before making any transactions.

1. Not doing your research – If you don't fully investigate the cryptocurrency you invest in, you cannot complain if that currency fails.

2. Mining – Don't think that going out and buying your own crypto mining rig and starting her up is going to make you rich. Mining requires massive amounts of electricity, and really successful rigs require huge amounts of computing power. So, unless you can afford a rig costing many 1000's of dollars and can then hook it up to a solar farm, it is probably not worth it. If mining is something that interests you and you'd like to give it a go without the hefty price tags, you can join a consortium and take out a stake in a large mining setup. These can be found by doing online searches. But beware, there are many crooks out there, so ensure you check them out thoroughly before handing over any money.

3. Holding your nerve – You may need to be brave and look at holding onto your coins for the long-term. It is easy to get spooked into making rash decisions to sell your coins when they experience a crash. Hold your nerve, don't be tempted to sell. Instead, give them time to mature and reach their full potential.

4. Private Keys – This is one of the biggest mistakes rookie investors make, not knowing their private keys. Hundreds of millions of dollars have simply evaporated into thin air because people didn't remove their wallet service

offline to somewhere safe, an offline wallet. If you don't do this you don't have full control and your coins can be stolen or the information lost.

5. Online communities – There are dozens of online crypto communities. They are collectively hugely knowledgeable. Their combined knowledge and expertise can really help guide you into making sound choices, but more importantly, help you to avoid making costly mistakes! You can also post questions on the forums to get helpful answers about anything you are unsure about.

6. Wrong wallet – Another easy mistake to make is to accidentally try to put newly purchased currency onto the wrong wallet. Wallets are generally designed to hold only one currency. If you hold several currencies on different wallets, it can be easy to mix up your wallets and try to put new coins on the wrong one. Doing this will result in disaster and the loss of your coins, so beware! Some wallets do support more than one currency, by they don't support them all, so check first.

7. Hard copies – Always keep hard copies of all your passwords and private keys etc. Print them off and store them somewhere really safe. If you lose these you have lost the currency they pertain to.

8. Exchanges – Ensure the exchanges you choose, have two-factor authentication. This will help safeguard your purchases. When you receive your restoration code, don't just leave it on your phone, write it down somewhere safe. If your phone is lost, stolen or replaced, you will have lost your restoration code too and may not be able to access the currency you have on the exchange.

9. Criminals – Due to the amount of money involved in cryptocurrency, it has inevitably attracted a large amount of

criminal interest. Do your best to check things out in all aspects before making any decisions. Keep in mind at all time that people are out to steal your money and take all precautions you can to safeguard it.

If you follow the steps above you can look forward to a fun and hopefully rewarding time investing in cryptocurrency. If not, then you could potentially lose any money you invest in it.

The Future of Cryptocurrency

While the relatively short amount of time cryptocurrency has been around making it difficult to chart its future, there are several different events taking place worldwide that give some clue, at least, into what the future of cryptocurrency could look like.

Increasing regulation: One of the key facets of Bitcoin at launch was the fact that it allowed for completely anonymous transactions to take place online. This, of course, led to countless illegal activities being perpetrated on the system, many of them, even now, centered around the Silk Road marketplace. Since this was first made known to the Department of Homeland Security, the SEC, FCN, and the FBI, they have been working on a case that may be close to finally changing the status quo of Bitcoin forever.

At the same time, the Federal Reserve is currently working on another solution to the same problem. In this instance, they would cut off the Bitcoin problem at the source by simply releasing its own cryptocurrency instead. It is tentatively called Fedcoin and sources near the Federal Reserve say that it is closer to reality than you might think. This is because all it would take is a simple fork of the Bitcoin blockchain, coupled with a new genesis block, to get the new cryptocurrency up and running.

Initially, Fedcoins would be easy to exchange for USD on a one to one basis, though eventually, it will likely be able to find places to purchase fiat currency. The biggest difference between it and other cryptocurrencies is the fact that the Federal Reserve would, of course, retain control over the blockchain which would give them the ability to create or destroy blocks at will. They would also be able to see all of the details surrounding every transaction, making Bitcoin's anonymity a thing of the past.

First national cryptocurrency: Proving once again that they are at the forefront of everything having to do with Cryptocurrency, China recently announced that they are on the verge of releasing their very own cryptocurrency, having already successfully completed tests between their central bank and other financial services. While many of the details remain unclear, the information that is already available points to a cryptocurrency whose blockchain can scale essentially as needed, regardless of the level of demand that is placed on the system. It is tentatively scheduled to come to market around the same time that the renminbi is released, though a precise timetable remains unclear.

This marks a major step, not just for China, but for the idea of national cryptocurrencies as a whole. It also shows just how committed China is to work through the inevitable technical and economic challenges. Regardless of how it all works out, it is undoubtedly going to have serious repercussions on the world financial system in more ways than one; not to mention showing the world just what a centralized currency can do.

It will also mark the first time that a digital currency has a value that is directly tied to a bank note which has the potential to decrease transaction costs associated with all types of transactions made with the currency. It will also mark the first time an estimated hundred million Chinese citizens will have easy access to banking services, adding a significant chunk of online sales to the mix as well.

The cryptocurrency will also give the Chinese government some means to control the growth of speculative cryptocurrency trading that has been going on in the country, essentially without any oversight whatsoever. It also will be interesting to see how having a local alternative will affect the Chinese appetite for Bitcoins and ether. The new currency is also going to give the government previously unimagined access to financial data and the related habits of its citizens as the currency is designed to be easy to track. This should help to cut down on the corruption China is currently facing in its banking sector as well.

Policymakers have also shown an interest in the insights that having access to all of this data will provide when it comes to motivating the local economy. The digital addition will also automatically make the renminbi more of a going concern as anyone in the world will be able to easily acquire and spend it, without having to deal with traditional exchange fees.

Conclusion

Thank you for making it through to the end of Rise of the Crypto-knights: The Fundamental Guide To Investing In Cryptocurrencies for Beginners. Let's hope it was informative and able to provide you with all of the tools you need to achieve your goals, whatever it is that they may be. Just because you've finished this book doesn't mean there is nothing left to learn on the topic, expanding your horizons is the only way to find the mastery you seek. The world of cryptocurrency is constantly changing at a dramatic rate which means if you don't keep up with the latest information you will be left behind.

Thanks for downloading this book. It's my firm belief that it has provided you with all the answers to your questions.

Thesaurus of Terms to Understand Cryptocurrency

ASIC, or Application Specific Integrated Circuit – ASIC mining is a pretty crafty method of mining various coins at a rate much faster than that enabled by any regular computer. ASIC is a chip, which is specifically created to execute one task. Enter ASIC mining. An example of one such model is an ASIC miner created to ONLY process SHA-256, which is the problem offered by the Bitcoin blockchain to mine new coins. There are also ASIC's for script which specifically solves the mathematical code in relation to altcoins such as Litecoin. Though in recent years there has been a good amount of dialogue surrounding the longevity of mining this way and we've even seen coins making it so that it's impossible to mine with an ASIC.

Address – a bitcoin address, which defines the location from which you would receive, send or hold your currency. This may be the same address as your home address. This is a long string of 26 to 35 alphanumeric characters, which look like:

3NhM1fqH3stf8LCL37k2FG7D5kpdQH3eTR

A wallet address is the public portion of the two encrypted keys necessary for a holder to accept or verify a transaction.

Altcoin – the accepted name of any coin that isn't Bitcoin.

Bitcoin – is the first cryptocurrency, which was created by Satoshi Nakamoto in 2009.

Blockchain – a type of distributed ledger, which digitally records unchangeable data in packages that are called blocks.

It is a full list of all the blocks that have been mined. Cryptography is the main operator that allows for users to engage with the ledger without the need for any central figurehead. In layman's terms, this means that people and computers all over work together to create a network instead of a network being made by one single person or company. This network is enabled and protected through cryptography. We have seen this used in currency, data transfer and on. The blockchain is comprised of "blocks" and is constantly growing as each new record, datum, or block is added to the chain for everyone to see.

Block Reward – a reward, which is given to a miner after successfully hashing a transaction block.

Confirmation – when a blockchain transaction has been verified by the network, it is called confirmation. A confirmed transaction, cannot be reversed or double spent.

Cryptocurrency – a digital asset used as a medium of exchange for purchases or services. It uses cryptography for secure transactions.

Exchange – cryptocurrency exchanges act as an intermediary to move money and cryptocurrencies between users and networks. Centralized bodies which transfer currencies between block chains and regular currencies are referred to as exchanges.

Fork – this means changing a cryptocurrency's software that will create two different version of the blockchain. Both these versions will have shared history.

Genesis Block – the first block in the chain. A genesis block will always have a height of zero because there is no block preceding it.

ICO (Initial Coin Offering) – just similar to **IPO**, where coins are offered instead of shares. If a new cryptocurrency project wants to raise fund for them, a particular amount of coins is offered to the public at price.

Ledger – a *distributed ledger* is an agreement of shared, replicable and synchronized data, which are spread across multiple networks, across many CPU's. A *central ledger* is used when all the data while being synchronized and replicable, are controlled by a singular network or individual.

Mining – the act of generating new bitcoins using computing hardware by solving cryptographic problems. Transactions are verified and added to a blockchain. A reward is given for solving the algorithm and lengthening the chain, which is called a mining reward. The mining reward for the Bitcoin blockchain is Bitcoin.

Node – a computer connected to the Bitcoin network. A node receives a copy of the full blockchain. It supports the network through validation and relaying of transactions while receiving a copy of the full blockchain itself.

Paper Wallet – a piece of paper print out that stores altcoins in a secure, off-line environment.

P2P – another way of saying Peer-to-Peer. Peer-to-peer has become a very large focus of blockchain as one of the biggest selling points is decentralization. Nearly every interaction on the blockchain can be fulfilled P2P, or without a centralized variable like a store, bank or notary. In peer to peer transactions, the blockchain is decentralized, so that transactions are faster and easier.

Public & Private Key – the public key is a cryptographic key that can be used by any party to encrypt a message. Another party can then receive the message and, using a key that is only known to that individual or group (private key), decode the message.

Satoshi – the smallest possible fraction of cryptocurrency named after the inventor which is available for transactions. It is approximately 0.00000001 BTC.

Smart Contract – a two-way smart contract is an unalterable agreement stored on the blockchain that has specific logic operations akin to a real-world contract. Once signed, it can never be changed. A smart contract can be used to define certain computational benchmarks or barriers that have to be met in turn for money or data to be deposited or even be used to verify things such as land rights.

Wallet –digital address, which is accessible through a private key in which cryptocurrency can be stored, sent or received. Software wallet is a storage for cryptocurrency that can exist purely as software files on a computer whereas hardware wallet is a device that can store cryptocurrency in the most secure way.

Whitepaper – documentation, which describes a cryptocurrency protocol in detail.

BONUS

I wanted to show my appreciation that you support my work so I've put together a free gift for you.

https://nb1publish.weebly.com

Just visit the link above to download it now.

Thanks!

Joseph Evans

Please, review this book

If you enjoy this book, would you please consider leaving a short review at the book's Amazon page. It helps others to make an informed decision before buying my book.
Thank you so much!

Copyright 2016 by Joseph Evans — All rights reserved.
All rights Reserved. No part of this publication or the information in it may be quoted from or reproduced in any form by means such as printing, scanning, photocopying or otherwise without prior written permission of the copyright holder.

Disclaimer and Terms of Use: Effort has been made to ensure that the information in this book is accurate and complete, however, the author and the publisher do not warrant the accuracy of the information, text and graphics contained within the book due to the rapidly changing nature of science, research, known and unknown facts and internet. The Author and the publisher do not hold any responsibility for errors, omissions or contrary interpretation of the subject matter herein. This book is presented solely for motivational and

www.ingramcontent.com/pod-product-compliance
Lightning Source LLC
Chambersburg PA
CBHW070211230526
45471CB00002B/921